T.U. Webb

Patriotism Without Partyism

T.U. Webb

Patriotism Without Partyism

ISBN/EAN: 9783337307790

Printed in Europe, USA, Canada, Australia, Japan

Cover: Foto ©Suzi / pixelio.de

More available books at **www.hansebooks.com**

PATRIOTISM

WITHOUT

PARTYISM.

Price. - - - - - Thirty-Five Cents.

PATRIOTISM WITHOUT PARTYISM:

OR,

AN OBSCURE MAN'S EFFORTS TO REDEEM HIS COUNTRY;

CONSISTING OF

THOUGHTS AND REFLECTIONS

SUGGESTED FROM TIME TO TIME BY OUR NATIONAL TROUBLES; AND ADDRESSED TO THE AMERICAN PEOPLE.

By T. U. WEBB.

SAINT LOUIS:

OGAN AND VIVIAN, PRINTERS, S. E. COR. SECOND AND LOCUST-STS.

1868.

PREFACE.

The author of this little book deems that the only preface which it needs, is a simple statement that the articles comprised in it were written at or near the time of their respective dates, and, with a few exceptions, were published in some of our public journals;—that he believes them to be more or less applicable to the present state of things in our country;—that he has never held an office, made a political speech, nor been a member of any political Convention or Caucus:—and that previous to the breaking out of the Rebellion, he was unaccustomed to writing for the Press.

Should any one wish to know the author's *politics*, they may be expressed briefly, in the following words: The greatest good of the largest number

In *morals*, he believes that, The way of the transgressor is hard; that innocence is better than repentance; and that to be good, is to be happy.

PATRIOTISM WITHOUT PARTYISM.

A CALL TO ALL HANDS.

March 23d, 1861.

MY FELLOW COUNTRYMEN:—We are in trouble. That noble ship, built and bequeathed to us by our fathers; consecrated by their toils, their suffering, and their prayers; is nearing the breakers. I hear the roar, and see the foam, of the billows. There is a mutiny on board. Our gallant Commander is about to make an attempt to restore order among the crew, and save the ship.

Let us lay aside all *party* feeling, and rally to his support. Without our united aid and sympathy to sustain him, and give strength to his arm, his efforts will be fruitless. The ship will go down, carrying us with it, into the abyss of irretrievable ruin.

Let us forget we were ever Republicans or Democrats, and fly to the rescue. Is not the object worthy of the sacrifice?

LOVE OF COUNTRY versus LOVE OF PARTY.

To the Editor of The N. Y. Tribune.

Illinois, April 2d. 1861.

Sir: The rancor and malignity exhibited in our political discussions for some years past, together with the critical condition in which we are now placed, have convinced me that it is extremely detrimental to the welfare of our people and the successful working of our system of government, to form political parties upon principles which bring into direct antagonism two interests so vital and dear as the Freedom of Conscience and the Right of Property.

Will you oblige a sincere lover of his country, and a devoted Republican, by publishing the above, with any comments which you may see fit to make.

Yours truly,

T. U. WEBB.

———

REPLY.

My Dear Sir: You have started rather a good idea—one very fruitful in its development. In order to give it logical scope, we must further stipulate that, whenever two nations engage in war, they shall use cornstalk swords, and never fire balls made of any harder substance than hasty pudding—that no man who "pitches into" one who has offended him shall do so till he has first covered his fists at least a foot deep with light cotton batting — that any one who gets the better of his neighbor in a bargain shall be careful not to make more than five dollars out of him — that no lady meditating matrimony shall understate her age beyond the term of twenty-four calendar months — and various kindred safeguards against evil consequences, whereof the mere mention would fatigue the general reader.

Knowest thou not, O, Webb! that this, into which we have been precipitated, is a right earnest world, wherein we must battle with obstacles as we meet them, hardly finding opportunity to boil the peas that from time to time drop into our boots, much less making asses of ourselves by insisting that all peas shall be grown ready boiled? For Nature has other ways of her own, and is quite as stubborn with regard to them as we are, being at the same time a trifle the stronger.

Parties do not make nor choose the political or other topics whereon mankind shall from time to time be arrayed in antagonism to each other — these grow irresistibly out of the progress of our race — or rather, they are divine instrumentalities looking to the gravest and most benignant ends. Many an honest, good-hearted Tory in our Revolutionary age (when there were as good men on the Tory side as on the other) thought it a great mistake that people did not go on fighting Indians, clearing up forests, catching fish and growing tobacco as of old, and let the King and Ministry govern as they thought best. They would have dearly liked some regulation whereby everybody should be constrained to pay whatever taxes Parliament might see fit to impose, and make no fuss about it — but you see that could not be.

You cannot frame a tariff, nor build a Pacific Railroad, nor (through the action of Congress) improve a River, nor clear out a Harbor, nor do anything else of the least moment, that does not seriously affect private interests, and so interfere, in some measure, with the Rights of Property. If you undertake, by regulating the sale of intoxicating liquors, to check by law the ravages of Drunkenness, you conflict materially with what are called Rights of Property; if you insist that loafers shall not play ball too noisily under church windows during Sabbath services, you are held to interfere with their Rights of Conscience. In short, O, Webb! this perverse world, in which you and I find ourselves, has not been got up on the principles which would have insured to it social tranquillity (but I think at grave cost) had you created it, and there is no course open to us but to take things as they are and try to make the best of them. Which is the course earnestly recommended to you by

Yours, &c., &c.,

ED. TRIBUNE.

REJOINDER.

To the Editor of the N. Y. Tribune:

DEAR SIR: I have the honor to acknowledge the receipt of your reply to my communication of April 2d.

You seem to have misconceived the purpose of my note, and the spirit in which it was written. I was merely trying to pour a little oil on the mad waters into which the nation was being plunged; not seeking to make it appear that the Republican party was responsible for the trouble that has come upon us.

Were I of that class whose faith and works are the opposite of yours, it would not be difficult for me to find in your reply, together with much that has appeared in the Tribune of late years, ample ground to justify the inference that you have been a little more willing to accept, than anxious to avoid, a civil war. But I will not judge you so uncharitably. I will ascribe to partisan enmity and political prejudice what your enemies have imputed to baser motives.

The compliment you have paid me at the outset of your remarks, I can reciprocate without flattery. You, likewise, have put forth not only one, but several good ideas; and expressed them in a manner that fully sustains your reputation. The idea of two nations engaged in war, using cornstalk swords, and firing balls made of no harder substance than hasty pudding, is equal to some of the best in Gulliver's Travels. The allusion to the Tories in our Revolutionary age, is another good thought, cleverly written out, and will be likely to exert a "healthy" influence on some of their descendants, who may have inherited the weakness of their forefathers. Covering a man's fists a foot deep with light cotton batting before he pitches into one who has offended him, is so closely allied to the gloves and practice of the pugilist that it seems to lack dignity and originality.

Perhaps the most objectionable passage in your reply is that wherein reference is had to a lady meditating matrimony, and a man getting the better of his neighbor in a bargain. Here you appear to have exposed yourself to criticism. Your language would seem to imply an elasticity of conscience, a sliding scale of morality, which I was not prepared to see exhibited by the Editor of the Tribune. If a lady meditating matrimony may understate her age without violating any of the moral principles laid down in the Decalogue, why should she be limited to the term of twenty-four calendar months? If, by understating her age forty-eight or seventy-two calendar months, instead of twenty-four, she would thereby be more likely to succeed in attaining the object of her desires, why not grant her the requisite indulgence? And if she may deceive her lover or her betrothed in regard to her age, why may she not, with equal propriety and innocence, deceive him in other things?

Again, if a man may get the better of his neighbor in a bargain without going counter to the precepts of Christianity, why should his cupidity and shrewdness be restricted to the paltry sum of five dollars? Why not let him "make a good thing of it," and get the better of his neighbor — if he can — to the amount of ten, fifteen, or twenty dollars; and so on *ad libitum?*

An experience of nearly half a century, on this mundane sphere, has convinced me that it is in truth, a right earnest world. Especially this part of it. Here, the great irrepressible conflict is waged on a scale, and with a method and constancy, that have no parallel in any age or country. Here, the wheel of fortune revolves with a rapidity that frequently turns the brain. He that was down yesterday, may be up to-day; and he that is up to-day, may be down to-morrow. Here, it is push, push, push along keep moving; and woe unto him that is not endowed with good propelling power. Here, whoever would make a noise in the world, must blow his own trumpet — but whither am I drifting?

One word about vegetables. If I am not misinformed, you have accumulated a respectable quantity of that which enables one to make the journey of life with his boots comparatively free of hard peas. I do not envy your good fortune. You have earned it by a life of industry and tact in the practice of your profession, and have a right to enjoy it. But had the Rebellion been the means of cutting off your business resources, and reducing you and your family to indigent circumstances, perhaps you would be better prepared to appreciate the condition of those who have experienced a similar fate.

With regard to "making assess of ourselves," I have only to say, in conclusion, that if you will agree not to make an ass of yourself by needlessly increasing the number of hard peas, I will agree not to make an ass of myself by insisting that all peas shall be grown ready boiled.

Respecfully yours,

T. U. WEBB.

THE SOLEMNITY, AND THE NEEDS OF THE HOUR.

June 11th, 1861.

A few weeks ago, the commercial metropolis of our country was visited by a young man in the bloom and vigor of manhood; of uncommonly prepossessing personal appearance, and the idol of a large circle of friends. The purpose of his visit was to enlist a military company; to aid in protecting our Government, and defending the city of Washington; the inhabitants of which, he said, were placed upon a volcano.

Having organized his regiment, the young man returned with it to Washington, and fell a martyr to his country's cause, and to his own self-sacrificing devotion to that cause. His body sleeps the sleep of death. His spirit has doubtless gone to commune with the spirits of the men who fell at Bunker Hill.

This whole Nation is now placed upon a volcano; which has been giving out all the premonitory tokens of an extensive and overwhelming eruption. True, there is at this moment a comparative lull in the war of elements; but it is the calm that fore-runs the convulsion; the stillness which precedes the last struggle of expiring nature.

Such being our condition, can we not be better employed than wrangling about who shall have the place made vacant by the untimely decease of the lamented Douglas, and contending about who shall be Speaker of the next Congress? Are we so accustomed to acting the part of political gladiators that we must needs continue our petty quarrels while the Nation is bleeding at every pore, and writhing in the agony of attempted suicide? Is this the part of wise men and patriots? Are we proving ourselves worthy custodians of a political heritage fraught with so many blessings, and purchased at the expense of so much precious blood and treasure?

Shade of Washington, of Warren, of Hancock,

of Adams, of Jefferson, of Jackson, of Webster,
and of Clay! come back and awaken your countrymen to a just sense of their danger and their duty!

A BRIEF POLITICAL SERMON.

June 16th, 1861.

When Nations become degenerate and corrupt,
like individuals, they need to be regenerated or
born again. If a man wax fat, and kick, he requires
chastening. Nothing does this more effectually
than a few lessons in the school of adversity.
This People having waxed fat, and kicked, are
being chastened. They are in the furnace of
affliction; and ere long, I trust, will be on the stool
of repentance; when we may look for reformation.

The germ of the disease, which has at length
reached the vitals of the Nation, was implanted in
our system. It has grown with our growth, and
strengthened with our strength, until the antagonism has become so deadly there must be a life-
and-death struggle between us and the disease.

Our Constitution being good, I trust we shall
outlive the malady, and be born again.

I hope, and fervently pray, that one of the first
effects of the new birth may be a purification of

the "pool of politics;" so that honest men and christians may "dabble" in it, if they choose, without getting "dirty."

For many years we have been more or less the tools and prey of political gamblers; who have made the Government and its emoluments the stake for which they have played. Hence, those who could not take part in the *gambling,* have had but a small share of the *winnings.*

But I trust a new era will yet dawn upon us; when the people, after being sufficiently ground between the upper and the nether millstone, will see and feel the necessity of employing men to wield the machinery of government who have some higher aim than a mere desire to enjoy the "spoils," and be "dressed in a little brief authority." God speed the day!

A SUGGESTION TO SLAVEHOLDING SECESSIONISTS.

June 30th, 1861.

To the Editor of the Charleston Mercury.

DEAR SIR: Will you permit me to tell you and your readers what I would do if I were a secessionist and a slaveholder? Instead of trying to break up this Union and Government, I would go to South America, seek some healthful and productive region wherein slavery is tolerated, purchase as much land as I had the means to cultivate successfully, remove thither with my family and slaves, and try to persuade my secession friends and relatives to do likewise.

OUR DUTIES AND RESPONSIBILITIES.

July 22d, 1861.

To the Officeholders, Officeseekers, Politicians, and Editors of Political Journals in the United States.

GENTLEMEN: The interests and destiny of this Nation are measurably in your hands, and under your control. Are you duly sensible of the momentous obligations and responsibilities which rest upon you at this fearful juncture of our public affairs?

If so, are you endeavoring to meet these obligations and responsiblities in a manner befitting their solemnity, importance, and magnitude?

Heretofore, the battles you have waged have been comparatively bloodless; and although the mode and spirit in which you have conducted the warfare have had a very pernicious influence upon the manners and morals of the people, yet their material interests, in the aggregate, have suffered no lasting, irreparable detriment.

Now, the scene is changed. From a conflict of opinion, interest, and passion, we have passed to a conflict of arms; from a war of words, to a war of blows; involving the destruction of human life, and the dearest ties that bind society together. That greatest scourge of nations, with its countless evils, and untold atrocities, has come upon us. No Mexican or Briton confront us now. Our foes are the descendants of men who fought shoulder to shoulder with our fathers, in the great struggle which achieved our national independence, and laid the foundation of the Republic.

It is our fate to behold what the great American Statesman and orator prayed he might not live to see. "A once glorious Union broken into dishonored fragments; States dissevered, discordant, belligerent; a land rent with civil feuds; and drenched in fraternal blood."

People! do you realize the vast change in the condition of our country, and the consequent necessity for a change in your habits?

Lovers and servers of Party! let me assure you the only party which the country needs in this dark hour of trial and disaster is a party of pure patriots, and upright statesmen.

Officeholders! while you are enjoying the honors and emoluments of your position, large numbers of your countrymen are being reduced to bankruptcy and ruin. Many a husband and father, who, a few short months ago, were in the possession of everything essential to the enjoyment of earthly happiness, are now passing sleepless nights and anxious days thinking how they may pay their debts, and keep their families from poverty and destitution,

Republicans! bear in mind that the cardinal principle on which you fought your way into power implies that you have a higher sense of right and wrong than they who opposed you; but do not, I adjure you, let the operation of this sense be limited to considering the African's wrongs.

Soldiers! remember that you live in the nineteenth century of the Christian era; and that you are fighting to save the Republic founded by Washington, Franklin, Hamilton, and their compeers.

THE RULING PASSION STONG IN DEATH.

August 20th, 1861.

I perceive that many of our people are still calling and holding Republican, Democratic and Bell-Everett meetings and conventions.

As an American citizen, deeply interested in what is now transpiring in our country, I would respectfully ask, For what purpose are these meetings and conventions being called and held?

Are we to have Republican, Democratic, and Bell-Everett brigades and divisions in our army? If so, I greatly fear the disaster at Bull Run will never be retrieved. In our *political* battles, excepting the last, wherein the people of the South were purposely divided, they have generally eaten us because of their unity, and our division. hall like cauces produce like results in our *military* attles? Are we of that class who will not learn, ven in the school of experience?

The Republic is in the agony of dissolution; early half its columns have been wrested from eir place; thousands of lives and millions of oney have been spent in trying to restore them; et a portion of our people continue to pull the ires and work the machinery of party, as though ere were nothing to fight for but the "spoils." ruly, the ruling passion is strong in death.

Must we go down with the words Party, Reublican, Democrat, and Abolitionist, ringing in our urs?

AN APPEAL FOR UNANIMITY.

December 7th, 1861.

I desire to address a few thoughts to those who ould have the Government emancipate and arm ie slaves in the revolted States.

A little more than a year ago, we were passing rough a violent political conflict; in which the ombatants were divided mainly into two parties, espectively styled Republicans and Democrats. he former had published to the world that the ading object for which they were contending, was to confine Slavery within its present limits; but not to interfere with it where it was already established by virtue of local law. The principal aim of the Democratic party seemed to be to oppose the Republicans; and among the most effective and frequently used weapons employed by them for this purpose, was the charge that the Republicans were Abolitionists; and that they wished to use the power of the Government to abolish slavery. The contest resulted in favor of the Republicans; whereupon, a portion of the people residing in the slaveholding States openly declared they would not submit to a Republican administration of the Government; and immediately set about making preparations to cast off their allegiance, and establish a separate independent government for themselves. The Chief Executive officer of the Nation having constitutional scruples with regard to the propriety of interfering in the quarrel, and the Democrats of the North continuing to rail at their successful rivals, the Revolutionists, meeting with no serious resistance, made rapid and fearful headway. So alarming had the state of things become at the close of the late Administration, that the friends of the President elect, fearing he was in danger of being assassinated, deemed it prudent to call out a strong military force to protect him, and preserve order during his Inauguration.

Thus rapidly were we drifting into the maelstrom of anarchy, when the Nation was electrified with the intelligence that Fort Sumter was being bombarded. Immediately the dormant patriotism of our Democratic brethren in the North "sprang into newness of life;" and when our new Commander called for help to suppress the mutiny, they responded nobly to the call. From that day to the present they have continued to swell the ranks of our army; to spend and be spent in the defense of their country and Government. Of the six hundred thousand men now in the field, I presume it is safe to conclude that one-half are Democrats; who, fifteen months ago, were bitterly opposed to the immediate abolition of slavery; and to everything tending to remove the social and political distinction between the two races. Think you these men have so far conquered their prejudices as to be willing to fight side by side with emancipated slaves, or engage heartily in the work of prosecuting the war for the abolition of slavery? Would it be wise, generous, or just, to make them the unwilling instruments to carry out a policy which they have heretofore opposed so strongly?

Countrymen! ye who make it your vocation to cater to the prejudices and appetites of your readers and hearers! ye who fan the flames and add fuel to the awful conflagration that is consuming us! ye who trim your sails to catch the breeze of every popular clamor! can you not distinguish between a civil war and a political campaign? Is your love of gain and your desire for self-aggrand-

izement so strong that you will trifle with the
destiny of your country in a crisis like this, for the
sake of a little short-lived popularity, or a few
dollars and cents? If you would have this fiendish conflict brought to a speedy conclusion; if you
would not have it protracted until every household
in the land shall be shrouded in gloom for the loss
of some one of its loved members; if you would
not have the people of the two sections worry and
tear each other until both parties shall be compelled
to desist, from sheer exhaustion, like two dogs
equally matched in strength and ferocity; if you
would not have them fight until they shall stand
aghast at the havoc and devastation which their
own hands have committed; if you would have
the horrors, the carnage, and desolation of this
bloody struggle confined to the States in which it
originated; if you would not give aid and comfort
to the foes we are combating; if you would not
extinguish the last ray of hope in the hearts of
those noble men who have sundered the ties of
blood and kindred, and in the midst of treason,
treachery, and persecution, have clung to the flag
of their country, and labored so earnestly and
efficiently in behalf of our cause; I implore you
in the name of all that is good, great, and sacred,
to abstain from agitating and discussing those
questions and subjects which tend to excite division and discord among the friends of the Union.
We need to be united in thought, feeling, and
purpose. A portion of those who were once our

political brethren have determined to pull down and destroy the fair fabric reared for us and them by our fathers. It is our duty to uphold and preserve it. Let us go forward in the work with an eye single to this great end; and see that we fall not out by the way. Let us prosecute the war to suppress the Rebellion, and restore the integrity of the Republic. If we do this with all our energy and resources, be assured, slavery will abolish itself quite as fast as we are prepared for it.

And while we are providing for and disposing of the slaves, let us do this in such a manner as will meet the approval of our own conscience, and least conflict with the prejudice of those who were once our political opponents, but now helping us fight the battles of our country.

Finally, let us remember that we are engaged in a war in which fathers are fighting against sons, sons against fathers, and brothers against brothers; that human nature and human passions are pretty much the same now as they were in the days of Robespierre, Danton, and Marat.

THE PRESIDENT'S INJUNCTION OBEYED.

January 30th, 1862.

In obedience to the injunction of our President, in his Inaugural Address, I, as one of his countrymen, have endeavored to "think calmly and well on the whole subject" of our national troubles — their causes and consequences. My reflections, with my reading, observation, and experience, have impressed me with the conviction that one of the greatest blessings which the Almighty could confer upon this nation at the present time, would be to take from us and our foes every dollar of money which we and they 'possess, and deprive us and them of all power to make or get more for a third of a century.

This would place us in a condition which, in my judgment, would be most favorable to a speedy reconcilement of our differences, and a return to peace and happiness.

REASONS FOR NOT BEING IN FAVOR OF ABOLISHING SLAVERY BY MILITARY POWER.

February 15th, 1862.

Having done what I could, in my humble way, to promote the success and sustain the credit of the Republican party, from its inception up to the present, I wish to state my reasons for declining to co-operate with that wing of the party which is apparently seeking to make the extinction of slavery the paramount object of the war, on the part of the Government.

I. It would be likely to drive from us all our (white) friends in the revolted States, and nearly half of those in the loyal States.

II. It would place us in great danger of having the seat of war transferred from the slaveholding to the free States.

III. It would be likely to plunge us into a state of anarchy, such as the world has never seen; from which we could be relieved only by a military Despotism.

IV. It would make fighting the chief business of the nation.

V. It would make us an easy prey to foreign Powers.

VI. If we should succeed in conquering the people of the slave-holding States, it would compel us to keep them in a state of vassalage more humiliating and degrading than that of their own slaves; thereby converting our Government into a monarchy; or a hybrid between a Republic and a Despotism.

VII. It would be likely to make the condition of large numbers of the slaves worse than it is at present.

VIII. It would verify the statements and pre-dictions of those who opposed the Republican party.

A PARABLE

NOT FOUND IN ANY OF THE BOOKS OF THE OLD OR NEW TESTAMENT.

March 3d, 1862.

And it came to pass in the days of Elijah the Tishbite, that the sons of Reuben the Hittite took unto them wives and went into a far country and settled.

And God prospered the sons of Reuben the Hittite, and blest the land wherein they dwelt; insomuch that they became a mighty Nation.

When their fathers had gone the way of all the earth, the children of the sons of Reuben the Hittite said, "We are wiser than our fathers:" and they quarreled among themselves.

And the Lord sent a great scourge upon them, which laid waste their fields and their cities, and destroyed many thousand lives.

And the people being sorely smitten, said unto their rulers, "Can't you work for lower wages?"

And the rulers said unto the people, "Go to, we love you dearly; and we love our beautiful country, and glorious Government."

After many days, when the fat of the land had been consumed, and the sorrows and burdens of the people began to press heavily upon them, the people again said unto their rulers, "Can't you work for lower wages?"

And the rulers again said unto the people, "Go to, we love you dearly; and we love our beautiful country, and glorious Government."

ANOTHER POLITICAL SERMON.

March 12th, 1862.

With the close of the civil war now raging in our country, we shall doubtless have turned over a new leaf in our National history. God grant that the record on the next page may be cleaner and purer than that on the last.

As a Nation we have much to regret, as well as much to be proud of. We have cause to be proud of our origin; of the wisdom, sagacity, and heroic deeds of our fathers; of the beneficent Government which they framed; of our unparalleled prosperity; of the general intelligence of our people; of the favored clime in which our lot has been cast; but, alas! we are not what we were.

Love of money, and the desire to be "dressed in a little brief authority," being two of the strongest passions of human nature, I presume that in all countries where the people choose thier rulers, there will be parties contending with each other for the privilege of managing the public affairs, and enjoying the money of the nation, vulgarly called the "spoils."

History teaches us that the feuds and animosities engendered by this contention for power and pelf between large bodies of men, are the rocks upon which the ship of state, in a Republic, is most likely to split. It would seem, therefore, to be the part of wisdom and exalted statesmanship to endeavor to soften the asperities, and mitigate the evils, resulting from this incessant partisan warfare. Such appears to have been the view entertained by our most eminent statesmen, for, from the formation of the Government up to a recent period, whenever our gallant ship got into troubled waters, there were men on board who could "take her latitude" in the darkest weather, and pilot her safely through the impending danger. Two of the last and noblest specimens of this class of men passed from among us about nine years ago; having worn themselves out in helping to work the ship through one of the most fearful storms which she ever encountered. The one had prayed that he might not live to see his country "rent with civil feuds and drenched in fraternal blood." God granted his prayer. The other was spared the pain of seeing his beloved State made the field of deadly strife between his friends and neighbors. Peace to the ashes, and honor to the memory, of these departed patriots. We ne'er shall see their like again.

Scarcely had the earth time to settle, and the turf become green, over the graves of these men, when the demon of [discord seems to have been let loose amongst us; for, ever since, we have been snarling and] snapping at each other like cats and dogs, until at [last we have got to shooting each other down by thousands.

Parties, then, being inseparable from a Republican Government, I would respectfully suggest that we endeavor to organize them hereafter on such principles as will not bring into violent collision the Rights of Conscience in one half of the Nation, and the Rights of Property [in the other half. Upon these two great interests, mankind, in all ages and countries, has ever been extremely sensitive and tenacious. Men have suffered martyrdom rather than violate their conscientious convictions; likewise, they have died in resisting what they deemed encroachments upon their rights of property. The bloody and desolating wars between the Catholics and Protestants originated from causes somewhat similar to those which have brought on our civil war.

If I can get a second, I will propose that we try to form a party, having for its objects:

First, The promotion of truth and justice, intelligence and virtue.

Second, An amendment to our national Constitution which will make the President eligible by the votes of the people alone; limit the number

of candidates for the Presidency at each election
to two; and provide for a choice of candidates as
follows :

About four or five months previous to the
time of holding a Presidential election, let the
people meet at their usual place of voting and
vote for their favorites; when these votes are all
polled and canvassed throughout the United
States, let those two men representing opposing
principles and parties, and having the highest
number of votes in their favor, be the candidate
for the Presidency; and in like manner select from
the rest the candidates for the Vice Presidency
This method of choosing candidates and electing
a President would supersede the necessity of
National Convention, wherein the people sometimes
have no voice nor choice in selecting candidates
and prevent a recurrence of the dilemma and em
barrassment resulting from the election of
President by a minority of the people.

'HE PARTY SPIRIT IN THE NORTH MORE DIFFICULT TO SUBDUE THAN THE REBELLION IN THE SOUTH.

April 7th, 1862.

'o the Editor of the Chicago Evening Journal:

DEAR SIR: I sympathize with you in your "reret" that party spirit should continue so rampant 'hile the nation is in such great peril and deep 'liction.   Ever since it became apparent that a ollision of arms between the people of the two ections of our country was inevitable, I have ex-ted what little ability God has given me in yiug to induce my countrymen to cease their arty bickering. But I am almost ready to give p in despair, being forced to the melancholy con-'usion that it will be far easier to conquer the ebels of the South than to subdue the party spirit f the North. I can see no remedy for this great vil but in a miraculous interposition of Divine 'rovidence.

How strange that, while our brethren of all political parties and creeds are in the field, fighting ide by side to suppress the Rebellion, and restore he Union, those who remain at home should per-ist in the manifestation of that spirit and feeling 'hich brought upon us our heavy calamities. Vhile one portion of our people are pouring out heir blood to extinguish the fire that is consuming is, another portion are equally sedulous in adding

fuel to the flames. While one man tells the people
of the South that we do not wish to interfere with
their slave property, another says that, "next to
the labors of William Lloyd Garrison, he deems
the labors of John Brown more valuable to the
country than those of any other American!"

THE BALANCE OF POWER IN A REPUBLIC.

April 15th, 1862.

There is probably no form of government in
use among civilized nations wherein the tendency
to rebellion, and the facilities for promoting it, are
so great as in that of a Republic embracing a wide
extent of territory divided into departments or
States, each having its own local government,
separate and distinct from that of the whole. For
the convenience of illustration, the two great
powers or forces of the social and political systems
in a Republic of this character may be compared
to those of the solar system; the State governments representing the centrifugal, and the General
government the centripetal power of the *political*
system. In the *social* system, the centrifugal power
may be said to reside in that large class of persons
consisting of office-holders, office-seekers, politicians,
and editors of political journals; those not in-
cluded in this class may be supposed to constitute
the centripetal power. The latter naturally inclines

to a state of rest or tranquillity: the centrifugal delights in motion and excitement; hence, avails itself of every expedient and occasion to keep the centripetal stirred up.

The centrifugal power may be subdivided into the "ins" and the "outs." Between the "ins" and the "outs," on all subjects relating to political affairs, there has existed from time immemorial an inveterate antipathy. Whatever the "ins" may do or propose to do, the "outs" hardly ever fail to condemn and oppose it. Consequently, whenever the political affairs of a confederate Republic are so managed as to throw the entire centrifugal power of a large section among the "outs," and there is a strong sympathy and community of interest between them and the entire centripetal power of the same section, a Rebellion and civil war will be likely to ensue.

THE SLAVERY OF PARTY.

May 28th, 1862.

We have seen much, and heard more, of the evils of African slavery, as it exists in our country; but there is a slavery prevailing among us which, in my estimation, is almost, if not quite, as prejudicial to the best interests of the Nation, as the bondage of the black man.

The latter is limited (at present) to about four millions of human beings, and confined to about one-fourth of the territory embraced in the Republic. The other is restricted to no lines of latitude or longitude; but extends from ocean to ocean, and from the Aroostook to the Rio Grande; from the pine forests of Maine and Minnesota, to the ever-glades of Florida, and the chapparal of Texas and Arizona. No class, no color, no station, is exempt from its influence. Its chains are felt alike by the occupant of the White House, and the humble dweller in the log cabin of the far West. The manner in which it operates, and the effects which it produces, are various and multiform. It distorts the vision, contracts the view, warps the judgment, and makes the whole man one-sided. It has alien-ated friends, divided families, broken up churches, and torn society into fragments. It has set brother to warring against brother, son against father, and father against son. It has caused our public men to degenerate from a race of enlightened, liberal, courteous, and dignified Statesmen, into a race of quarrelsome politicians, and greedy spoilsmen. It has converted our halls of legislation into arenas for the exhibition of spleen, passion, and gladiato-rial combats. It has perverted our public journals from being — what they should be — the hand-maids of truth, justice, and intelligence, into vehicles of slander, abuse, and misrepresentation. It has impelled men to magnify the sins and errors of one-half their countrymen, and wink at the iniquities and transgressions of the other half; to revile and traduce one class of their fellow-citizens, and pander to the passions and prejudices of another class. It has frequently excluded our best men from office, and put in our worst. It has withheld from a Webster and a Clay the honors which they earned so nobly, and bestowed them upon men who were greatly their inferiors.

Its galling yoke must be worn, its humiliating requirements must be rigidly and vociferously complied with, by all who would exercise any influence in public affairs, or enjoy the slightest morsel of the "spoils."

To the enslaved black man there may come a year of Jubilee; for the victims of this other form of servitude there would seem to be no hope of relief but the Millennium.

Reader, would you know the name of this species of slavery? It is the slavery of party; and the bigotry of political opinion.

A NEW IDEA.

May 12th, 1863.

Eureka! After long and anxious reflection, I have arrived at the conclusion that the best way to effect a permanent adjustment of our national difficulties, and re-establish our Government on a firm basis, would be to divide the people into two parties; make the number of each as nearly equal as possible in every State, Territory, County, and election precinct, throughout the Republic; assign to each party an equal share of office-holders, office-seekers, politicians, and editors of political journals; then make it the organic law of the Nation that no office in the Government, from that of President down to that of a Town Constable or country Squire, could be filled for two consecutive terms by a member of the same party. In other words, whenever any officeholder's term of office expired, let his successor be chosen from the opposite party. This would equalize the distribution of the "spoils;" moderate the rancor of party strife; and stimulate our public men to work for their country and the whole people, instead of a party. Who will help to set this ball in motion, and thereby hasten the political Millennium?

ANOTHER APPEAL FOR UNANIMITY.

July 30th, 1862.

It has been affirmed by one whose judgment and patriotism are entitled to high respect, that the Union, if restored at all, must be restored as it was. To restore the Union as it was in the palmy days of the Republic, when our Senators and members of Congress could discuss questions of public policy and express their differences of opinion and feeling in a manner befitting their high position, and the great interests entrusted to their charge, "would be a consummation devoutly to be wished;" to effect which, the little that remains of one poor life would be willingly sacrificed.

But to restore the union as it was, we must "make that not to be which has been." We must call back the departed spirits, reanimate the lifeless forms, of those who have fallen in this demoniac strife.

We must replace the amputated limbs, and repair the shattered frames, of its living victims; silence the wail of widows and orphans, the shrieks and groans of the wounded and dying; and root out from the hearts of a maddened people the bitter hate, the fiendish malice, begotten by this inhuman conflict. Without the power to perform these miracles, it were vain to talk of restoring the Union as it was. We might almost as well think of restoring the entombed cities of Herculaneum and Pompeii as they were.

Scarcely more feasible, in my view, "would be the attempt to separate, and form ourselves into distinct Nationalities. For, God and Nature have so arranged our country — at least that portion which lies east of the Rocky Mountains — that it would seem to be our manifest destiny to live together as one people, whether our Government be a Republic, a Monarchy, or a Despotism.

What, then, shall we do to suppress the eruption from this volcano of human passion which is desolating our fair land? How shall we extricate ourselves from the mad vortex in which we are plunged; and escape the still lower depth to which we are tending? How shall we bring back the halcyon days of peace?

Muzzle the Abolitionists, says one. Many of us have been trying to do this for years; but the more we try to muzzle them the more clamorous they become. Like the ghost of Banquo, they will not down at our bidding.

Abolish slavery, says another. Abolish slavery! Undo the work of two centuries! Annihilate an institution that existed in our country before we were born as a nation; which had fixed itself so deeply and firmly as to baffle the efforts of the framers of our Government to place it in course of extinction; which has grown with our growth, and strengthened with our strength! Make a sudden and radical change in the life-long social relations and relative position between ten millions of people on the one hand, and four millions on the other! Convert men into a belief that that is not property which they have been accustomed all their lives to regard as property! Eradicate the combined influence of education, habit, and pecuniary interest! Strike the shackles from four millions of Africans diffused over an area of more than 700,000 square miles, while ten millions of Anglo Saxons are determined to keep them on! Suddenly elevate four millions of men, women and children from a state of the most abject dependence and degradation, to a position of self-reliance and freedom from restraint, for which they have not had the slightest preparation!

Countrymen! let us not imitate the folly and madness of the Rebels. Let us not lose all by attempting too much. Slavery is dying quite as fast as we are prepared to have it die. Let us not be so eager to hasten its death as to destroy ourselves with it.

Again the great question recurs, what shall we do to be saved? How shall we re-unite a divided people? How shall we re-establish law and order where anarchy reigns supreme; and avoid the dire necessity of erecting a military Despotism over the ruins of nearly half the Republic? In the language of the immortal Webster, how shall we reconstruct the fabric of demolished Government? These are the momentous questions—"big with the fate of empire"—which present themselves

for our consideration. Who can answer them? I
will not make the attempt with my weak brain
and limited attainments.

There are a few suggestions, however, which I
will venture to express. They whom we are
fighting are united by the cohesive power of a
common interest, and energized by the hope of independence. We are not united, but have our
energies weakened, and afford aid and comfort to
the Rebels by our differences and dissensions as to
what caused the war; how it should be conducted;
and how the Government should be administered.
They are consolidated. We are divided into Con-
servatives, Republicans, Democrats, and Abolitionists:
each faction or party seeking to have the Rebellion
suppressed and the unity of the Nation restored in
accordance with its own peculiar views and wishes.
If it be true that in union there is strength, then
the Rebels possess one very important element of
success which we lack.

Americans! descendants of patriot sires! lovers
of freedom! friends of the Union! if we would
speedily crush the Monster which has risen up to
blast the goodly work of our fathers; if we would
preserve what cost them so much to achieve; if we
would perpetuate the American Republic; if we
would carry our Government triumphantly through
the severe ordeal which has come upon it, and
make the great heart of humanity, of civilization,
and of progress, beat with a quicker pulse; we

must relinquish our partisan views, prejudices and predilections; bury the animosities of party; throw overboard our platforms; and work together for our country's good on the broad level of patriotism; in the spirit of conciliation, concession and compromise. What! compromise with Traitors and Rebels ? By no means. Compromise with ourselves, with each other, and with the loyal people of the South. Emulate the spirit, and heed the dying admonition, of the departed Douglas. "Sacrifice party upon the altar of country." If we do this, if we will but adopt this spirit and policy, I think I can assure you that our noble ship of state, which has been so long on her beam ends, will right up once more; her sails again fill, her broad pennant stream out, and be hailed with joy by every lover of freedom throughout the civilized world.

But if all parties factions and persist in clinging to their respective platforms, and insist upon carrying out their peculiar views and principles; if we continue to feed and inflame each other's passions and prejudices; to wrangle and bicker, abuse and misrepresent each other; to irritate, provoke, exasperate, and "pitch into" one another, as we have been doing for years past; if we have such an itching for notoriety, and cheap distinction, that we cannot refrain from giving utterance to language and sentiments that shock the nerves and wound the sensibilities of the nation; if we con-

tinue to be impatient at the slow progress of the
world, and over zealous to make it move faster?
I fear the war will continue until the Republic
shall have crumbled into chaos.

Then, tyrants will rejoice and their subjects weep.
Then, "Freedom will shriek, and Hope, for a season,
bid the world farewell." Then, "bitterer tears will
flow than were ever shed over the remains of
Grecian or of Roman art," for we shall have destroyed "a more glorious edifice than Greece or
Rome ever saw." Then, the Genius of Liberty
which accompanied our fathers across the ocean,
and cheered and sustained them under their pri-
privations and toils, will drop a tear over the
tombs of her beloved Washington and his com-
patriots, and flee to the Alpine peaks and more
congenial atmosphere of the land of William Tell.

But let us hope for better things. Let us work
and pray for the regeneration of our afflicted
country; and endeavor to hasten the advent of
that auspicious era, when men can be free without being licentious; and when the proud bird
of our national ensign, like the fabled Phœnix, risen
from its own ashes, with eye undimmed, and plu-
mage unsoiled, shall again spread his protecting
pinions over a peaceful, united, prosperous, and
happy people.

To Hon. Horace Greeley, Ed. N. Y. Tribune :

August 26th, 1862.

DEAR SIR: Presuming that I am one of the twenty millions of people whom you assumed to represent in the prayer which you recently offered up in their behalf, I wish, respectfully and briefly, to set forth my reasons for declining to say amen.

I. In my judgment, it lacks two of the most essential ingredients of a good prayer; viz: humility and faith.

II. I think it violates that commandment which says: "Thou shalt not bear false witness against thy neighbor."

III. It seems to partake of the leaven of the Pharisees; who uttered long prayers in the synagogue, and at the street corners, that they might be seen and heard of men.

IV. It breathes not the spirit of charity; without which, the apostle Paul assures us, we are "as sounding brass or a tinkling cymbal."

V. You appear to forget that our Government is a Republic; that the President is not invested with unlimited powers; and that the people of the loyal States do not all look from the same stand-point; nor hate the Rebels and their peculiar institution with the same degree of intensity.

VI. I am one "of those who triumphed in the election" of our present Chief Magistrate; and "desire the unqualified suppression of the Rebellion now desolating our country." But I am *not* one of those who "are sorely disappointed and deeply pained by the policy he seems to be pursuing with regard to the slaves of Rebels." He has not yet forfeited my confidence, nor my respect. Though I think he has committed errors—among which is the reply to your "prayer"—nevertheless, I will not forsake him, nor judge harshly of his motives; but, so far as I have the ability, will endeavor to strengthen his hand, encourage his heart, and aid him to discharge the momentous duties and responsibilities which devolve upon him in this dark hour of national woe and peril.

A CHANGE OF POLICY AND OF STRATEGY PROPOSED.

September 18th, 1862.

To the loyal people of the American Union:

BRETHREN: I address you in behalf of an agonized Republic and a distressed Nation. "Hear me for my cause."

For nearly eighteen months we have been waging a conflict that has sent probably three hundred thousand of our fellow-citizens into eternity; diseased, demoralized, mutilated and crippled a number equally large; carried grief and mourning into many a household; devastated large districts of our country; and impoverished the nation to an extent that is frightful to contemplate. Notwithstanding these vast sacrifices and severe afflictions, this copious "blood-letting," and this enormous depletion of our finances; and notwithstanding that we have greatly the advantage of our foes, not only in the righteousness of our cause, but also in numbers and resources; with every inlet and outlet of their coast guarded by a Navy that has no superior, and but few equals; with seven hundred thousand men in the field, of the best blood of the Anglo Saxon race; well paid, well fed, well clothed, and well armed with the most improved implements of death; and abundantly supplied with the best munitions of war the world affords; after nearly eighteen month's fighting, the rebellion still rears its Gorgon head more defiantly than ever.

What, and where, is the malign influence that mars our success, and impedes our progres? Is it the "border State eunuchs?"* Then let them "slide," and make way for men that are not emasculated. Has the President "not a spark of genius, and no enthusiasm?"* Let him resign and his place be filled by a man of larger calibre, and more mettle. Are our Generals incompetent, and unfit for their stations? Dismiss them and try others. But my purpose is not to find fault, nor cast reproach. This would be emphatically a work of supererogation. My object is higher, and holier. I have a change

---

* These expressions are quoted from an editorial article which appeared in the New York Independent.

of policy and of strategy to propose, by which I think we can conquer. It is peaceful and humane. It will receive the favor of Heaven, and command the sympathy of the good and true. It will be twice blessed — blessing him that gives, and him that takes. It is easy of execution. The only serious impediment to be overcome is prejudice. Who will not conquer his prejudices to save his country? Mine are conquered, and they were strong. Hitherto, so far as slavery was affected by this contest, I have been more conservative than otherwise. Not because I did not think slavery a great social, moral, and political evil; not because I sympathized with Traitors; but, because I was anxious to avert and mitigate the horrors of war. But conservative ground is fast disappearing beneath the bloody waves of this devilish strife. Its angry billows are fast closing in upon me, and I must prepare to meet them. I must take a more decided stand either in favor of the interests of Freedom, or in favor of the interests of Slavery. Distasteful as it may be, I must draw nearer to the Abolitionists of the North, or nearer to the Traitors of the South. The decision is made. I have chosen the former alternative. Every instinct of my nature, and every impulse of my heart, are loyal to Freedom. I see clearly that, henceforward, the American Republic or its bastard offspring must be the ruling power of this great Nation. The constitutional rights of slavery and of slave-holders, in my view, are growing beautifully less. The obli-

gations that once bound me, bind me no longer.
They have raised their parricidal hands to destroy
the glorious fabric which my forefathers aided to
rear. By the help of God they shall not succeed in
their diabolical design. I see that Freedom or Slavery
must die. They are having their last grapple. Freedom must triumph.

"The eternal years of God are hers."

People of the non-slaveholding States, and soldiers
of the Federal army! whenever you grow tired of
this "unnatural and unnecessary" war, and wish to
see it brought to a speedy conclusion, just conquer
your prejudices, and say to the bondmen and bondwomen of the Rebels, "Come ye over the border."

Fear not that they will become our equals, or that
we will become their equals. "Can the leopard change
his spots, or the Ethiopian his skin?" Who would
not rather see these degraded and oppressed Africans
diffused over the free States of the North, than see
the Rebels triumphant and our Government overthrown? Besides, they can be deported and colonized
just as well from the free States as from the slave
States.

"Sink or swim, live or die, survive or perish," let
us not ingloriously fritter out our national existence;
but if we must die, let us die speedily, and gloriously
defending the sacred trust committed to our keeping
by the sages and heroes who founded the American
Republic! *Vive la Liberte!!*

"The combat deepens.   On ! ye brave,
Who rush to Freedom, or the grave."

"Thrice is he armed who hath his quarrel just."
Watchman, what of the night?   Pilot, how do you
head?

ON THE PROCLAMATION.

October 9th, 1862.

By announcing that he will proclaim freedom to
the slaves of all slave-holders who shall be in rebellion
against the Government on the first of January next,
our President seems to have made himself the subject
alike of unmeasured obloquy and fulsome panegyric.
I am not prepard to participate in either of these
"demonstrations."   The sovereign power of this Nation
resides in the people, and the President, in the position
which he at present holds, is merely an agent employed by the people, for a limited period, to perform
the functions pertaining to one branch of the Government, of which he is but an individual member.

We commenced our national existence with two
conflicting elements incorporated in our social and
political fabric.   Whatever may have been the immediate cause of our troubles, or whoever may be
to blame, the antagonism between these elements
has been made to culminate in civil war; one part
of the nation having rebelled, and the other part

being obliged to resist the rebellion. In the course of the struggle, a seeming majority of the people who have remained loyal to the Government — or at least a majority of those who are loyal to the present administration of the Government — have informally signified that they wish the President to do what in their opinion he has a clear right to do, and what they think will greatly facilitate and expedite the crushing of the Rebellion. Having given the subject due consideration, the President announces that if the rebellion be not subdued within a specified time he will accede to their wishes; which, in my judgment, makes him neither a demi-god nor a demon.

If the President were possessed of Almighty power, he could free the slaves in the same manner that God sent light into the world; but being a mere mortal, like the rest of us, he may say, "LET THE SLAVES BE FREE" as often as the Muezzin exclaims that Mahomet is the Prophet of the Lord; yet, unless the mandate be properly sustained and executed by the people, it were better addressed to the slaves of Brazil.

To the Editor of the Chicago Evening Journal:

October 17th, 1862.

In the editorial columns of the Chicago Tribune, of October 15th, the following statement appeared:

"The Tories profess to be terribly shocked that any contra-bands should come into this State. But we notice that wherever a Tory can pick up a nigger he does so. The Republicans generally will have nothing to do with them."

For the credit of humanity, and especially that class of humanity called Republicans, I fervently hope they will not let their political opponents outdo them in benevolence to the poor escaped slave.

THE CONFLICTING ELEMENTS IN OUR SOCIAL AND POLITICAL FABRIC.

November 30th, 1862.

The founders of this Republic were, perhaps, the wisest statesmen, the purest patriots, and the most unselfish body of men the world has produced. But they were human, and had to contend with difficulties that were above and beyond the control of human agency. They had to frame a Government for a people in whose social fabric were interwoven discordant and conflicting elements, tending in opposite directions, and producing antagonistic influences. The one tending to universal freedom, social and political; liberty of speech ond of the press; and the general diffusion of knowledge among all classes and conditions. The other tending to an aristocratic state of society, and a monarchical form of Government; an abridgement of the freedom of speech and of the press; and the formation of classes with exclusive rights and privileges.

I think that a careful reading of our national Constitution, together with the discussions that were held upon certain of its provisions while it was being framed, will convince any impartial and disinterested person that the extinction of one of these elements was confidently anticipated by a majority of its framers; and that the instrument was framed with a view to this end. But owing to causes not then developed or foreseen, this element has not become extinct; but, on the contrary, has increased in vitality and power to such an extent that it threatens to extinguish the other element.

Arouse ye, then, my countrymen, and prepare for the great work before you. Let us make this the model Republic for future ages, and oppressed humanity in all climes.

HOW, AND WHEN, OUR TROUBLES WILL END.

December 12th, 1862.

How, and when, will our civil war terminate? is the great problem which is now attracting the attention of the civilized world.

Though neither sage nor prophet, nor the son of a prophet, I will nevertheless attempt to furnish a basis on which some vague opinion may be formed with regard to the probable duration of our national troubles. The people of the United States are divided into four great classes, or contending parties; one of which is distinguished by the name of Rebels; a large proportion of whom are armed with deadly weapons, and fighting — they say — to maintain their rights, and achieve national independence. Arrayed against these is another party, about equal in number, and equally well supplied with the means of destruc- tion, who are fighting to conquer the Rebels, and re- subject them to the authority of that Government which they are seeking to overthrow.

The other two classes — more bellicose than bellig- erent — profess to have a common aim; to wit: the sustaining of the Government; yet quarrel incessantly about the manner of sustaining it. In tenacity of purpose, vigor and venom, these combatants are not excelled by their more daring brethren upon the battle field. Their weapons are mainly the tongue and pen. Their mode of warfare partakes largely of the Guerrilla; such as discharging shots from masked batteries, firing under cover, shooting poi- soned arrows, and making raids upon the defenseless.

Now, whoever can compute the length of time, and the amount of suffering and slaughter that will be necessary to bring these contending parties into such a condition that their various conflicting opinions, interests, and passions, may be reconciled and har- monized; or tell when either of them shall have become strong enough to subdue the others, and hold them in permanent subjection, can tell how and when our civil war will be brought to a close.

THE CONSEQUENCES OF DISUNION.

January 8th, 1863.

About forty years ago, our Government deemed it proper to announce what has been termed "The Monroe doctrine;" one sentence of which reads as follows : " We owe it, therefore, to candor, and to the amicable relations existing between the United States and the Powers of Europe, to declare that we should consider any attempt on their part to extend their system to any portion of this hemisphere, as dangerous to our peace and safety."

Soon after the flames of civil war had burst forth among our people, the Governments of England, France and Spain, discovered that their interests in Mexico could not be suitably cared for without resorting to the diplomacy of the sword. Influenced, probably, by the consideration that in union there is strength, or perhaps from motives of political economy, these three Powers appear to have formed an alliance for the purpose of mutually assisting each other in the prosecution of their respective claims against the Mexican Government. Accordingly, a fleet, adequate to the emergency, was conjointly fitted out by them, and dispatched to the waters of Mexico. The unsuspecting Mexicans not having been duly advised of their coming, were not prepared to receive their distinguished visitors in a manner befitting the occasion. Suffice it to say, the Allied Powers effected a landing without having to overcome any very formidable resistance. Hardly were the troops disembarked, however, when England and Spain apparently abandoned the enterprise, and withdrew their forces. What impelled these two nations to do an act so unheard of in the annals of war; whether Mexico promptly redressed their grievances; whether they found that the end would not justify the means; whether they could not co-operate in harmony with the Emperor of the French; or whether they got ashamed of the work in which they were engaged, has not been made known to the world. Whatever the motive may have been, these two Powers appear to have receded from all active participation in the pending conquest of Mexico. Not so Napoleon. He continues to push his aggressions with renewed vigor; and, if our public journals tell the truth, draws largely upon the resources of this country for the ways and means to carry out his designs. We are also informed — through the same channel — that the Government of Mexico, through its representative at Washington, has complained to our Government that we are not acting with due regard to the principles of international comity; in brief, that we are not doing unto Mexico as we wish others to do unto us. In what spirit this remonstrance from the Mexican Government has been received, and what influence it may have on the future action of our Government and people, we have yet to learn.

Is there not reason to apprehend that this Nation has fallen from the proud position which it once as-

sumed so fearlersly, and maintained so firmly? Are
we deterred from dealing justly with a sister Republic because she is weak and her adversary is
strong? Is the gold of the French Autocrat so
tempting that we must gratify our cupidity at the
expense of the Nation's dignity and honor?

He that crushed the budding hope of his own
country, and placed his iron heel upon the Genius of
French Liberty, is now driving his blood-stained
car over the land of the free; and, sad to relate, we
seem to have become his passive instruments.

A QUERY PROPOUNDED.

January 20th, 1863·

President Lincoln has given freedom to about three
million slaves in the revolted States. A large proportion of the citizens of the loyal States, declare that
these emancipated Africans shall not come into their
presence.

Query: If we compel the people of the South to live
among freed slaves, and refuse to let freed slaves live
among us, will not this be a despotic exercise of
power?

February 5th, 1863.

In my opinion, the attempt to enlist, arm and equip, three hundred thousand negroes, and use them as soldiers on the field of battle in fighting the Rebels, as is proposed in the bill now being discussed by Congress, will tend to demoralize the Army, sink the Nation deeper in the vortex of anarchy, and disparage our claims to the respect and sympathy of foreign Governments.

If the officers of our army are invested with ample authority to employ negroes in any capacity which, in their judgment, will best subserve the cause in which we are engaged, where is the necessity for proposing and discussing this measure?

February 12th, 1863.

Ours being a Government of the people, deriving ;ts power from the consent and cheerful acquiescence of the governed, if I were asked for advice with regard to the general management of our public affairs during the fearful crisis through which the Nation is passing, I would say in reply, Strive to pursue that policy, civil and military, which is best calculated to secure the support of a majority of the people, and meet the approbation of the civilized world.

www.ingramcontent.com/pod-product-compliance
Lightning Source LLC
Chambersburg PA
CBHW022035080426
42733CB00007B/839